ORANGE

Elfchen Poems

Also by Pushpa R. Menon

UNEARTHED: Poems that Unearth (2025)

Pushpanjali : A Collection of Poems (2024)

Lore and More: Narratives of Kerala (2024)

ORANGE

Elfchen Poems

Pushpa R. Menon

Published by Cogitabund LLP, India
publishing@cogitabund.com
www.cogitabund.com

ORANGE: Elfchen Collection

A Cogitabund Book/ published by arrangement with the author

ISBN: 978-93-49383-19-7

Typeset and Cover Design by Cogitabund LLP

Contents

Dedicated

To all my poetry loving friends, who believe in the dictum

'*the briefer, the better*' in Poetry

ORANGE

Elfchen Poems

Foreword

The Elfin Charm of Pushpa Menon's Elfchen Poems

An athletics aficionado cannot be faulted for preferring steeplechase to marathon; a dance devotee, for appreciating Kuchipudi more than Bharatanatyam; or a connoisseur of arts, for pitching rule-bound traditional poetry above free verse. The levels of stamina, skill and intrinsic genius required for gaining excellence in these areas may be similar but it is an indubitable fact that the greater the challenges built into an activity, the more varied the talent needed to attempt it, the stricter the self-discipline to be followed to master it, and the sharper the expertise demanded to elevate it. Like steeplechase or Kuchipudi, rule-bound poetry is a difficult taskmaster. Poet-aspirants have to possess many attributes: core strength of expansive vocabulary, suppleness of rhetorical muscles, dexterity of rhythmic cadence and the ability to put on an impressive display of fresh perspectives.

The elfchen, a sub-genre of traditional poetry, is challenging in that it insists on poets maintaining strict adherence to its five-line, eleven-word form to convey their ideas, paint their pictures, express their emotions, establish their arguments or present their philosophies in a manner that is complete, clear and, preferably, new. This calls for a willingness to shave off lengthy and baroque segments, however fascinating they may be; enormous patience to chisel each miniature unit to a spartan finish; and enough cleverness to leave certain things unsaid so as to woo and sustain the readers' active interest.

Pushpa R. Menon's *Orange*, a staggering collection of 111 elfchen poems, possibly the first of its kind ever to be published, is a treasure box of miniature verse-gems. It is the child of an odd couple, a maverick dreamer who knits gossamer fabrics out of her imagination and a strict umpire who enforces a disciplined format for each piece with military precision. Her medium, the English language, lends itself, putty-like in her creative hands, to be compressed to convey a profound subject, stretched to develop an argument, braided to present multiple ideas, and sculpted to make figures. And she employs an impressive range of techniques to make such exquisite verbal filigree work – similes, metaphors, personification, alliteration, synesthesia, irony, defamiliarization, transferred epithets and so on. The result is that *Orange* gifts its readers with simple observations about life, word pictures of natural scenery and objects, personal perspectives on certain phenomena and social commentary on a range of issues. The minimalist sleekness and precision of the elfchen poems is further enhanced by their neat categorization under three heads, alliteratively titled "Elements," "Expressions" and "Essences".

The very first poem "Apples" is a tour de force where Pushpa straddles a huge swathe of time – from the ancient

OT age to the current AI age – with the lines: "Eve to Steve,/ Sun on sins shone," thus effortlessly presenting the whole race of humanity as monsters of greed, whether they reside in a pristine, God-crafted garden or occupy a Godless technology lab. If "Apples" deals with a single, condensed idea, "Ecstasy" shows how the same elfchen structure, however small, has enough maneuverable space for a wordsmith to start with an idea and move to its very opposite!

Ecstasy.

Loving you,

Building trusted ties,

Broken bridges of sighs,

Agony.

A similar algorithm plays itself out in "Sky" which leads the readers, step by step, from the sky to the clouds, thunder, lightning, rain and finally the earth!

Certain elfchen poems, like "Bangles," are fascinating, descriptive artefacts:

Bangles,

Coloured chimes,

Molten glass wires,

Melt in licking fires,

Branded.

While others, like "Eggs," with their heterodox perspective, are reflective pieces that provoke the readers to think deeply, cast off their tendency to take things for granted, and become more sensitive:

Life painted white.

Served on conscience platter.

Nipped.

In a rare piece like "Homes," the five lines of the elfchen, if detached from the title, read like a riddle:

Houses,

People build,

For restful sleep.

Wrapped in loving care,

Sheltered.

Pushpa Menon uses this poetic vehicle to convey her distress over various issues affecting humanity, like contamination of natural resources, destruction of the environment, growing violence, uncontrolled greed and so on. They make for powerful social commentaries. "Trees," for instance, exposes the hideous, self-destructive nature of humans whose rapacity has made them utterly short-sighted:

Trees,

Axe's greed.

Felled like giants,

Earth gasping, gritting teeth.

Freeze.

She also conveys her liberal views of philosophy through these tiny pieces. One of them is particularly evocative. Titled "Heaven," it presents four phrases that indirectly ridicule the conventional concepts we have of heaven as a divine sanctuary in a faraway realm:

Heaven,

Green earth,

Carefree innocent childhood,

Hearts where Gods dwell.

Serenity.

Another, titled "Love," pithily captures the central philosophy of all religions:

Love,

Is measured,

Only by love,

Selfless service without expectations.

Sublime.

From *Pushpanjali*, her first poetic offspring, to *Orange*, her second (though separated only by a year), Pushpa Menon has come a long way, and undergone a drastic, delightful metamorphosis. Emotional outpourings, copious in the earlier collection, have been stemmed; the fondness for purple prose has decreased; the anxiety to reach the reader, that unconsciously reveals itself through tautology, has ebbed; and the urge to dabble in rhymes and rhythm has lost its edge. *Orange* showcases a poet who is surer of her craft, and more trusting of her readers. This has given birth to a diction that is spartan yet subtle, a tone that is objective yet warm, and a style that is tight-knit yet free-flowing. These new features lend an elfin charm to her poems, and will surely provide an enthralling experience to her readers.

Radhika Menon

Rtd HoD of English, FMN College, Kollam

Preface

Why the title *Orange?*

In certain rare kinds of oranges there are eleven segments known as carpels. The eleventh one is a tiny, almost hidden one. Though this not true of all oranges, this image felt poetic with a quiet extra edge, much like an elfchen. I chose *Orange* for a title for its semblance with the elfchen structure as well as for it sparkling visual and taste-based associations. Oranges are also suggestive of vitality, warmth, tang, sunset, ripeness, even bitter sweetness – themes that echo in many of the poems. *Orange* is a metaphor for the ordinary made poetic.

Orange is a curated collection of poems written in the Elfchen form — a poetic form of five lines with a 1-2-3-4-1-word count structure. It was born from a desire to say less, but feel more and began as a quiet and joy-filled exercise in observing the world. The word 'elfchen' in German means diminutive of eleven. With its strict five-line, and minimal word count of eleven, it offers both a challenge and a quiet joy. It taught me to trim language down to its essence, to listen to the spaces between words, and to notice the poetry hiding in the most ordinary of things like rust, decay, fork, egg, rope, chair, breeze etc. The poems explore the way certain words lean into each other. They touch upon the elements, expressions and essences of everyday life. Themes of Nature, self-reflection, growth, survival, silence, selfhood, inner conflict, liberation, life, loss, love, and the power of small moments find a place in these tiny elfchens. Some poems use personification and contrast to provoke emotional and philosophical engagement. What connects them all is a deep trust in the small and the subtle. The intersection of word and image make ample room for contemplation. The five-line poetic form, lends itself to brevity, clarity, and restraint. The illustrations that are paired with each poem are designed to enhance the meditative quality of the book. Each image becomes a metaphor, each poem a mirror to hold up a thought, memory, or mood. I am grateful to Nishad SS, my go-to friend, for all technology related assistance and for so beautifully and aptly compiling the illustrations generated by Chat GPT, Freepik and Pintrest.

It is hoped that this book will bring you moments of recognition, surprise, or stillness. I am sure these five-line verse will linger and resonate with you.

Pushpa R. Menon

ELEMENTS

Apples

Apples.

Summer treat.

Eve to Steve,

Sun on sins shone.

Green.

Birds

Birds.

Feathered beauty.

Claiming the skies,

Unfurling flights of fancy,

Unbeaten.

Breaths

Breaths,

Drawn in,

Seek impossible goals.

Horizons blur unreached... unreachable.

Spurned.

Cherries

Cherries.

Blossom pink,

On shiny leaves,

Like brave, bold, beautiful,

Women.

Crows

Crows,

Darkly perch,

On waters clear,

Sullied, frenzied, unseeing, gaze,

Yonder.

Dark clouds

Black,

Dark clouds,

Shrouded in grief.

Night skies whimper soft,

Rumble.

Dawn

Dawn,

Breathing love,

Scattering silver smiles,

Earth draped in gold- green,

Divine.

Death

Breath,

In gasps,

Moments blur,

Then air stands quiet,

Stillness.

Decay

Decay.

Mud moans,

Pristine purity lost,

Scent of happy tears.

Petrichor.

Dusk

Dusk.

Sea breathes,

Sleepy summery breeze.

Ruthless ripples drift still.

Peace.

Fire

Fire.

Burnished ember,

Flamboyant yet tender,

Warmth reduced to ashes,

Strife.

Fishes

Fishes,

Glide gracefully.

Birds spy sly,

Peck, pick, stealthily fly.

Dependence.

Flowers

Flowers,

Heady fragrances,

Making air richer,

Whispers with the wind,

Bird songs.

Fruits

Fruits,

Orchard treats.

Myriad insects breed.

Bats, rats ravenous feed.

Fruitless.

Giant Millipedes

Unobtrusive,

Giant eco-beings,

Foraging rot unseen,

Measured steps on fabled legs.

Millipedes.

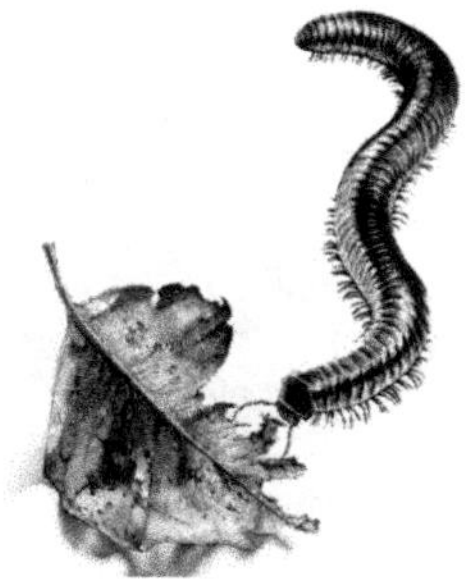

Grapes

Grapes.

Frown dark.

Purple pesticide jewels.

Sly, like death, lurking.

Lethal.

Heart

Heart,

Most compassionate.

Gentle, cool brooks.

Words warm with kindness.

Benevolence.

Honey

Honey,

Liquid gold,

Oozing sweet nectar,

Squeezing the hive dry,

Exacting.

Islands

Islands,

Severed connections.

Walled-in sad silences.

Striving to build bridges,

Forever.

Jasmines

Perfume,

Nano packed.

Slender capsules green,

Shining silver white sheen,

Jasmines.

Leaves

Leaves,

Diamond shaped,

Tears of trees.

Shed, yellowed in winds,

Weep.

Lemon

Lemon.

White, pink-tinged,

Perfumed, waxy petals,

Birthing tangy, sunny orbs.

Fruitful.

Light

Light,

Filters through,

Doors of heart,

Breeze breathes deep fragrance.

Liveliness.

Mangoes

Mangoes-

Yellowed pulp-

Like kindness spread,

On withered smiling lips,

Illumine.

Moon

Moon.

Curvy smile,

Brightens the blue,

Darkens to shine anew.

Brilliance.

Night Queen

Orange-lipped,

Teary petals,

Sun-drenched they fall,

In love, coral-shrouded, small.

Night queen.

Oranges

Oranges.

Some elfchen-like,

Have carpels eleven,

Ringing juicy, sweet bells,

Luscious.

Rhythm

Rhythm.

Systemic beats,

Singing until dark

Songs of the lark.

Stops.

Rivers

Rivers,

Never reverse.

Keep pressing forward,

Like life's pebbled flow,

Gurgling.

Showers

Showers,

In summer,

Nature's honeyed delight.

Make cool the night.

Bliss.

Sky

Sky,

Nimbus clouds,

Roar in thunder.

Spindly shards flash red.

Drip.

Smoke

Smoke,

Ash grey.

Drugs, dust, drought,

Knocked in comatose sway,

Faraway.

Sun-blushed

Sun-blushed,

Morning beckons.

Birds on trees,

Laughter shies coral red,

Flushed.

Sunrise

Sunrise.

Smiles play,

On Earth's lips,

Blossoms breathe petalled fragrance.

Awakening.

Trees

Trees,

Axe's greed.

Felled like giants,

Earth gasping, gritting teeth.

Freeze.

Water

Water,

Nature's ambrosia.

Creatures live, thrive.

Man spews plastic venom,

Derangement.

EXPRESSIONS

Ambitions

Ambitions,

Fly high,

Groping the sky,

Crushed in Time's crotch.

Dreams.

Anemochory

Whispers,

Soft melodies,

Whistling winds carry,

Into boughs of leaves.

Anemochory.

Anger

Anger,

Scorching heat,

Raging dry leaves,

Furious, untamed, menacing breeze.

Angst.

Apology

Apology.

Tiny word,

Sets wrongs right,

Lips tremble, shut tight.

Forgiving.

Beginnings.

Beginnings.

Brimming over,

With promises sweet,

Reached for the stars.

Fell.

Benevolence

Benevolence,

Caring hands,

Not piteous tears,

Restore fellow grieving hearts,

Steadily.

Beyond

Beyond,

Human greed.

Omnipotent nature sees,

Forests wrecked, bleeding seas.

Furious.

Communication

Communication,

Connections collapse,

Conversations curt, constrained,

Channels callous, cold, contained,

Chasm.

Earthquakes

Earthquakes,

Night piercing,

Wrath or wraith,

Earth staggers. Trees shatter,

Havoc.

Ecstasy

Ecstasy.

Loving you,

Building trusted ties,

Broken bridges of sighs,

Agony.

Gloom

Gloom.

Gathering darkness,

Sky silvery blue,

Awaiting my garden bloom,

Green.

Greed

Greed,

Cursed humanity,

Craving beyond need.

Tiny morsels, scarce feed,

Unconcerned.

Hatred

Hatred,

Drops precarious,

From our skies,

Screaming red in furious

Bloodshed.

Heaven

Heaven,

Green earth,

Carefree innocent childhood,

Hearts where Gods dwell.

Serenity.

Hell

Hell.

Summer floods,

Heat and wild fire,

Collapse of ocean currents,

Dissolution.

Hope

Between

Yesterday's regrets,

And tomorrow's promises,

Hide today's silver lines.

Hope.

Hypocrisy

Hypocrisy,

Sweeps out,

Like slashing wind,

Fine threads that weave

Intimacy.

Joyful

Joyful,

Whispers breathe,

Misty mornings sing,

Dusky eves solace bring.

Grateful.

Kiss

Kiss,

Intense emotion,

Sealed in love,

Sentiments awash, drinking deep,

Sweet.

Learning

Learning,

Tireless flame,

Unveils dark shadows,

Ushers in wisdom's glow,

Timeless.

Life

Life,

A race,

Twice run over,

Pursuing truth and love.

Endlessly.

Love

Love,

Is measured,

Only by love,

Selfless service without expectations.

Sublime.

Memories

Memories,

Bitter-sweet deep,

Moments snap sharp,

In fleeting seconds seized.

Undone.

Peace

Peace,

Blown asunder,

Innocence brutally murdered.

Mother Earth ruthlessly dismembered.

Alas!!!

Purity

Pure,

White lotus,

Disengaged from land,

Blushes pink on river-sand.

Detachment.

Red

Red,

Colours spread,

Hibiscus, poppy, blood,

Petals like tears shed,

End.

Reflections

Reflections,

Inner quest,

Through silent introspection,

Leaving footprints on Time.

Aligned.

Secrets

Secrets,

Sinister vine,

A strangling rope,

Twisting trust like knife.

Bloodless.

Sighs

Sighs,

Pressure outlets,

For raging skies,

Easing hearts, in red

Spread.

Speed

Speed,

Adrenaline spikes.

Busy roads standstill,

Dark, deep red flows.

Silence.

Surrogacy

Surrogacy,

Sowing seeds,

In alien lands,

Sheltering shade, setting sun.

Oneness.

Survival

Survival.

Drifting apart,

Freedom from stress,

Breaking away from ties.

Evolution.

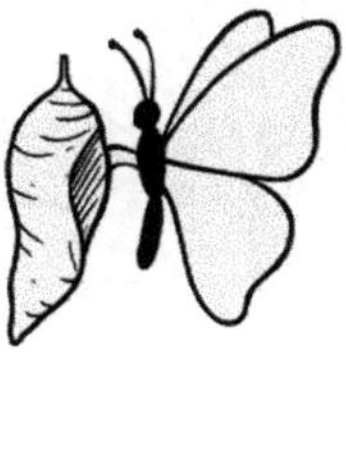

Symphony

On

Shimmering trees,

Wind whispers softly,

Laughter rustles russet leaves.

Symphony.

Temptation

Temptation,

Runs along,

The curved arch,

Of one's arms thrown,

Carelessly.

Terror

Terror,

Strikes blindly,

Blood spills hatred.

Skies, trees, human lives

Grounded.

Violence

Violence,

Blood strewn,

Lunacy let loose,

Omnipresent monsters spitting venom,

Chaos.

War

War-wrecked,

Dreams burnished,

Cold among blossoms.

Blind terror strikes mad.

Fatally.

Worship

Worship.

Divine powers.

Seats of spirituality,

Omnipresent immortal celestial bodies,

Within.

ESSENCES

Album

Photographs,

Trap moments,

In colour prints.

Eyes blur, pictures gather

Mist.

Baggage

Baggage,

Loaded with

Grievances of past,

Hang heavily on heart,

Hurting.

Bangles

Bangles,

Coloured chimes,

Molten glass wires,

Melt in licking fires,

Branded.

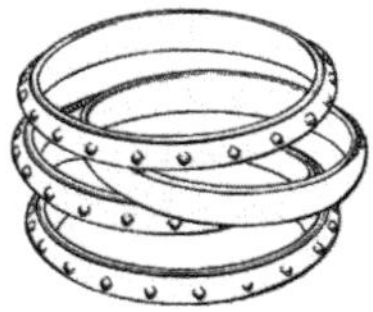

Books

Books,
Celebrate life,
Blurring infinite borders.
Parched minds and hearts
Quenched.

Chairs

Chairs,

That lull

One to sleep,

Spell total chaos when

Rocked.

Clocks

Clocks,

Like ants,

Tick forward marching,

Rest dream-like in sleep.

Alarming.

Clothes

Clothes,

Frilled fancy,

Adorning the wealthy.

For the threadbare, necessity,

Irony.

Dreams

Dreams.

Fitful feverish.

Eyes vacant, glazed.

Tears in fear trapped.

Lifeless.

Eggs

Eggs.

Yellow eyed.

Life painted white.

Served on conscience platter.

Nipped.

Fork

Fork.

Split roads,

Or pronged cutlery.

Each destined to shape

Choices.

Friends

Friends,

Lend solace,

When darkness enfolds,

Radiating starry smiles sublime.

Blessed.

Homes

Houses,

People build,

For restful sleep.

Wrapped in loving care,

Sheltered.

Humans

Humans,

Must recognise,

Compassion sans corruption,

Brings peace on earth,

Always.

Knife

Knife.

Culinary tool,

Or murderous weapon.

The hand speaks all,

Bluntly.

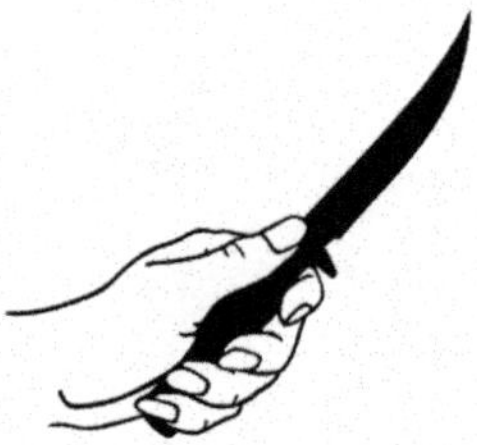

Lamp

Lamp.

Tiny speck,

Shines amber bright,

On the darkest night.

Unwavering.

Lines

Lines,

Paired straight

Drift endlessly away,

On seamless routes astray,

Estranged.

Mirrors

Mirrors.

Stand tall.

On the wall.

Reveal ravages of time.

Reflections.

Mother

Mother,

Largesse incarnate,

In warmth hides.

Where language and life,

Reside.

Pages

Pages,

Turn silent.

Her story speaks,

Of love's loveless streaks.

Unsmiling.

Palette

Palette.

Vibrant colours,

On one board.

Unity in diverse hues.

Solidarity.

Pen

Pen,

Mighty sword,

Inked passions flow,

Words in cascades glow,

Truth.

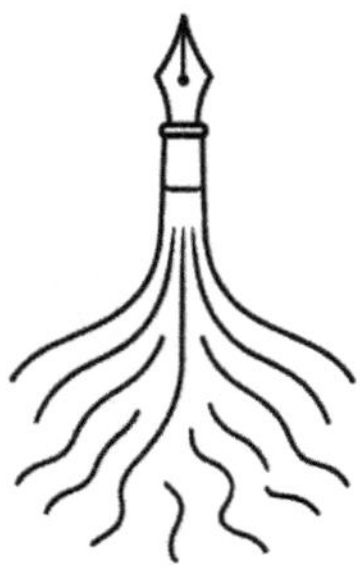

Photographs

Photographs,

Capture moments,

Etched in memory,

Ruffles up greying hair,

Fleetingly.

Pillars

Pillars,

Raised columns,

Of solid rock.

Sentinels of silent strength,

System-support.

Religion

Religion,

Diverse creeds,

Rooted in beliefs,

Converge at one point.

Acceptance.

Roads

Roads.

Trees bleed,

Green blood spills,

Black ribbons pretend grief,

Complacence.

Rope

Rope,

Tangled undergrowth,

Mixed coloured riot,

Unravels silk, softly spun,

Hope.

Rust

Rust,

Golden brown,

Like molten sun,

Flaky, freckled, frayed, futile.

Desire.

Screens

Screens

Mute conversation,

Create silent walls,

Stifle intimacy, leave relations

Fractured.

Spark

Spark.

Tiny light,

Licking away darkness,

Words fellow poets write,

Succinctly.

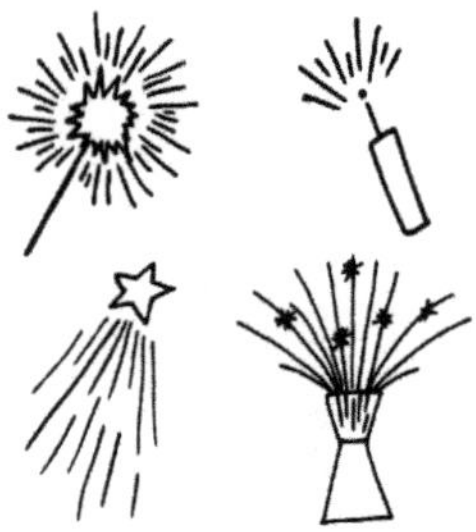

Stack

Stack

Care-worn baggage,

In nature's lap.

Travel through life's journey,

Light-hearted.

Stones

Stones,

Jagged, weather-beaten,

Lashed, washed ashore,

Mould into polished, rounded,

Pebbles.

Suppurations

Suppurations,

Buried deep,

Angst refusing sleep,

Secrets scars singeing grief,

Scathing.

Thrones

Thrones,

Vanity seats,

Powerful, poised, proud,

Leave one dazed when

Toppled.

Time

Time

Laughs quietly,

Carves deep furrows.

Buried silences linger long,

Passes.

Unity

Fingers.

Tightly knit.

Five in hand.

Weave into one fist.

Fortified.

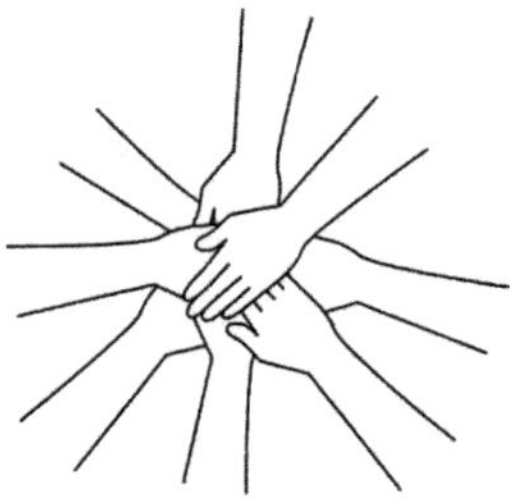

Walls

Walls,

Unlike bridges,

Create stone barricades.

Silences plastered, grievances smothered,

Circumvented.

Words

Words,

Reveal all,

Tumble and fall,

Crushed, overcome or stalled.

Lost.

www.ingramcontent.com/pod-product-compliance
Ingram Content Group UK Ltd.
Pitfield, Milton Keynes, MK11 3LW, UK
UKHW021400190726
13845UKWH00028B/780